Decorating with Family Photographs

creative ways to display your treasured memories

Decorating with Family Photographs

creative ways to display your
treasured memories

Ryne & Teresa Hazen

Sterling Publishing Co., Inc. New York
A Sterling / Chapelle Book

Chapelle:

Jo Packham, Owner

Cathy Sexton, Editor

Staff: Marie Barber, Ann Bear, Areta Bingham, Kass Burchett, Rebecca Christensen, Brenda Doncouse, Dana Durney, Marilyn Goff, Holly Hollingsworth, Susan Jorgensen, Barbara Milburn, Linda Orton, Karmen Quinney, Leslie Ridenour, Cindy Stoeckl, Gina Swapp

Photography: Ryne Hazen and Kevin Dilley for Hazen Imaging, Inc.

If you have any questions or comments or would like information on specialty products featured in this book, please contact Chapelle, Ltd., Inc., P.O. Box 9252, Ogden, UT 84409 • (801) 621-2777 • (801) 621-2788 Fax

Library of Congress Cataloging-in-Publication Data

    Hazen, Ryne.
       Decorating with family photographs : creative ways to display your
    treasured memories / Ryne & Teresa Hazen.
          p.   cm.
      "A Sterling/Chapelle book."
      Includes index.
      ISBN 0-8069-4211-8
       1. Photographs in interior decoration.   I. Hazen, Teresa.
    II. Title
    NK2115.5.P47H39   1999   99-35627
    747'.9--dc21   CIP

10 9 8 7 6 5 4 3 2 1

Published by Sterling Publishing Company, Inc.
387 Park Avenue South, New York, NY 10016
© 2000 by Chapelle Ltd.
Distributed in Canada by Sterling Publishing
c/o Canadian Manda Group, One Atlantic Avenue, Suite 105
Toronto, Ontario, Canada M6K 3E7
Distributed in Great Britain and Europe by Cassell PLC
Wellington House, 125 Strand, London WC2R 0BB, England
Distributed in Australia by Capricorn Link (Australia) Pty Ltd.
P.O. Box 6651, Baulkham Hills, Business Centre, NSW 2153, Australia
Printed in Hong Kong
All Rights Reserved

Sterling ISBN 0-8069-4211-8

dedication

To our loving parents,
whose example and never-ending support
have given us the confidence and
abilities to make this book a reality.

Ardus, Dale & Gayle — We love you.

acknowledgments

We wish to thank Jo Packham, owner of Chapelle Ltd., for this opportunity. Jo has been a business partner for many years and her friendship, trust, faith, and unending patience has allowed us to share our ideas with you.

We would also like to thank the entire staffs of both Hazen Imaging and Color Pro Lab for their dedication, enthusiasm, and hard work in seeing this project through.

In addition, we wish to acknowledge our colleagues who so graciously donated some of the sample images that appear in our gallery section and throughout this book. These fellow professionals are true artists and great image makers. Their talents and generous willingness to participate in this endeavor are greatly appreciated.

Last, but not least, we extend our appreciation to the following companies for their contributions: Artist Touch Framing, Exposures®, and Strauss Peyton Imaging.

about the authors

Ryne, a professional photographer for over 18 years, owns and operates three successful businesses in the photographic industry. In addition to his studio, he operates a custom photographic lab and digital imaging center.

Ryne's award-winning style of photography is well known throughout the area. With the growth of his businesses, he now only shoots on a limited schedule. His remaining time is focused on business management, education, product development, and the training of three associate photographers and his staff.

Teresa, an entrepreneur from an early age, started her own dance studio at the age of 18. After selling her business and marrying Ryne, she applied her skills at Hazen Imaging as a photo stylist responsible for make-up, hair, posing, and set design. She is currently involved in the development of several new concepts for Hazen Imaging. **Elements**© emphasizes high fashion teenage photography and the new **Legacy Series**© introduces high-end "concept portraiture" photography that includes the way in which the photograph will be styled, shot, finished, framed, and displayed.

contents

introduction

After having been involved in the photographic industry for over 18 years, Teresa and I feel there is a need to share some of our ideas on decorating with photography since it is an area that is so rarely addressed. We believe that when people use and display their precious photographs in their homes, fond remembrances are given new life.

We always try to emphasize to our clients how a beautiful photograph that is thoughtfully framed, creatively and properly hung, and viewed in the right light can be a welcome and decorative addition to any home.

By using your photography — be it a portrait, a landscape, or even a snapshot — to decorate with, you are able to "scrapbook" the walls of your home and tell the story of your life in a way that reflects who you are. Our goal is to help you see how your home reflects those qualities. When decorating with creatively styled and displayed photography, you can create a home filled with memories and love that invites all who enter with a warm welcome and sense of family.

Throughout this book, we will share many ideas with you on ways of doing just that — from classical and traditional styles to eclectic and sometimes "off the wall."

We all live in a "visual" society. We are suggesting to you that by taking your photographs and placing them on your walls instead of in an album or scrapbook, they will not only beautify your home, but allow you, your family, and your friends to enjoy them everyday. We have long seen posters, prints, and other art pieces sold as decor for homes. Many of these images are photographic in nature, so why not have these images be your own?

With the proper choice in photographic style or by creating your own images, you can capture and display your memories in a way that best portrays your life-style and taste.

We encourage you to remember that photographs play an important part of our lives. They are the windows of the past and the keys to our memories. Using them to decorate gives us the opportunity to enjoy and share the happiness and beauty they hold.

Let us begin ...

Treasured family photographs are so important, why not make your favorite the very center of your room? This photo was enlarged to 30 x 40 and used above this stone fireplace. When family or guests enter this room, their attention immediately travels to the simply mounted, but magnificent "piece of art" on the fireplace mantle.

In the deserts of Palm Springs, this home-decorating style is very much a combination of western and southwestern. This family surrounds itself with treasures they have discovered that are hand-crafted by artisans in the area. They also choose to accentuate their decorating style with small eclectic groupings of family photographs and keepsakes.

element one

determining your decorating style

The purpose in determining your decorating style is merely to give you a compass with which to guide you when selecting existing photographs or in creating new ones, which you will use in your new decorating scheme.

First, determine your decorating style by evaluating your personal style in the architecture, furnishings, and mementos in your home. Is it country, classical, contemporary, art deco, European, eclectic . . . .

decorating to suit your personal style

Treasured photographs are not always pictures of family members. They can be those images which were taken by different family members during an unlimited series of experiences. This family traveled extensively together in the countries of Peru, Bolivia, and Argentina; and so loved the images of the people there that they had these prized "frozen moments in time" enlarged, dramatically framed, and hung in the family dining room. It had to be the dining room — a place of importance that would remind each one daily of the moments and the memories they had lived and shared.

Arch De Triumphe - Paris, France
October 1997

Whether it is daily routine or a special event, the activities that fill your hours from morning until night become a part of you. Family photographs should be taken throughout the days. Whatever the occasion, the snapshots should be displayed where they are constant reminders that regardless of where you are or who you are with, time shared with family and friends should be remembered and enjoyed by everyone.

You may find that within your home you have several different styles or combinations of decorating styles. Each style can be accented and highlighted with photography that is representative of that style.

For example, your son's room may be decorated in a *&^$@#!?~* style, which may dictate using photographic images that are less rigid and nontraditional. In this case, why not take the pictures of his team and mount them on his headboard.

Your formal dining room, obviously more traditional, may lend itself to a more seriously stylized portrait of your family.

decorating
to suit your

life-style

Second, determine your decorating style by evaluating your life-style. You will want to decorate in a manner that portrays who you are and what you do. Is your life-style active, casual, career-, sports-, travel-oriented . . . .

You may find you have many different life-styles, depending upon the size of your family. Part of your days may be filled with your daughter's piano lessons and soccer games, your son's karate classes and tennis lessons, your spouse's off-road racing and gourmet cooking, and your own involvement in local charities.

decorating to suit your

Third, determine your decorating style by evaluating the display style of the photographs that tell the story of your life. Is it eclectic, organized, casual, formal, traditional, contemporary, accented by other objects, affected by lighting, determined by size or shape . . . .

You may find that you like displaying your photography in a combination of styles. For example, a single, large portrait contrasted by numerous small, individually framed "snapshot" type photographs hung together.

display style

"Works of art" are oftentimes purchased because of their unusual or unexpected qualities. It is, however, just as easy to take everyday cherished items and display them in a unique way that draws the attention they deserve. Here, a simple plate rack was used to display not only an heirloom plate, but cherished family photographs that bring too much joy to keep confined to the pages of the family album.

In contrast to the small snapshot-style photos displayed on the plate rack is this single large portrait hung over an office cabinet. Hung in a traditional manner, yet in a nontraditional office setting, it adds a loving feminine touch to a sometimes sterile space.

15

element two
decorating ideas and techniques

You have now determined all that is necessary to begin decorating with your family photographs.

It is important to remember that choosing to decorate with family photographs makes a statement about who you are. You will find that sitting in a room filled with family photos captures memories of times shared, portrays the people you love, and retells the special events of your life.

Creatively displaying these treasured memories warms the heart and fills the soul.

decorating

For some, the family pet is as important to the family as any of the other "human" members. They are loved, they are worried about, and they are missed when the family goes on vacation. It is, therefore, understandable why it is important to photograph the nonhuman member of the family, either with other family members or by themselves. These are the perfect pictures to hang in a man's study or the family room. It is probably the only picture the entire family will like!

on the wall

TO LOVE AND BE LOVED IS THE GREATEST JOY IN THE WORLD.

Traditionally, hallways have been a popular place for the hanging of family photographs. Here is a great example for displaying photos of generations. Using an untraditional matting and framing concept, these photos are simple, yet striking, virtually telling a story with each one. Dramatic lighting adds to the intensity of the subject matter.

It is such fun to decorate with frames of all shapes, sizes, and uses. This purchased bulletin board was made to hold pictures on both sides. In place of putting the pictures on the front of the refrigerator, they can now easily be taken in and out of this hand-painted frame.

Pictures do not always need to be hung on walls — they can hang anywhere! Try hanging an outdoor photo on a seldom used coat rack by the hall door. It can be hung with ribbon, jute, or even small chains. If you put what you love in unexpected places, they will be noticed and appreciated.

scrapbooks on the walls

Favorite photographs of lovers, family, or friends need not be framed to be hung on the wall — why not use them as wallpaper? In these rooms, very different techniques and types of photographs were used to literally cover the walls with memories. Selected pictures were reproduced on photo-quality paper then adhered to the walls with wallpaper paste.

create
memories

This wall was painted first, then stenciled with "frames." Pictures were chosen, cut to fit, and placed inside the stenciled frames.

Some photographs are so very special they deserve to be the center of interest in any room. This picture was accented by painting the entire wall with a background that complemented the picture. It is an unusual treatment that will delight any child or adult!

It has never before been so easy to creatively display favorite family snapshots. These frames are hung on the walls of a family cabin. They are pieces of barnwood held together by aged metal strips. Frames such as these are available to fit any decor and any life-style, whether rustic, formal, or just plain bright and colorful!

In addition to frames coming in every shape, size, and material, matting is also available in a wide variety of sizes and materials. In today's decorating, mats come in all finishes, from narrow one-inch borders, traditional, as well as oversized mat edges.

It is easy to forget that pictures can be hung on anything — not just directly on the wall. Here a shaker-style pegged rack is used — not for hanging traditional pieces of clothing, but treasured snapshots and favorite pieces of "art" clothing. There are many such objects from which to hang photos — how about hat racks, pegged wainscotting, or the front of a closet door?

When taking your your pictures in to be framed, be aware of the different effects that matting can have on your pieces. These pieces have been matted to develop a design style that is both unique and effective. A large mat and a small photograph make a statement of interest and importance.

What is more sentimental than a small replica of grandma's favorite quilt with old family photographs used for quilt blocks? Pictures taken in an earlier day of your grandma with her grandma and great aunt are perfect to display on the wall of a guest room and the quilt blocks are easily made. Photo transfer materials are available at most crafts stores and the instructions are simplistic. If you do not quilt yourself, your local fabric store can connect you with a quilter in your area who can complete your nostalgic piece of art.

Some family memorabilia is just simply too treasured to put in a box or a drawer to be remembered and shared only on special occasions. By using a popular "shadow box" framing technique, you can combine photographs and other memorabilia. The shadow boxes can be filled with pieces from the past — like lace from grandma's wedding dress or grandpa's watch; or today's mementos, like game tickets or a high school graduation tassel. The shadow boxes can be arranged vertically or horizontally to create the illusion of one large framed piece. An option would be to separate the pieces, space them as desired, and arrange them individually. Before actually hanging the pieces on the wall, arrange them on the floor until you have achieved the desired effect.

31

There are so many ways to take and display photographs. Don't forget that it can be the perfect idea to take three of your favorite shots taken during the same photo session and hang them together in a grouping. It need not always be different photographs taken on different days. Sometimes it is just too hard to choose which is your favorite, so why not use all of them. Hang them in a grouping, hang them in a row, or hang them in a "U" shape around a window.

Trendy in decorating today are individual "shelving" strips which are used to display photographs and collectibles. They can be hung singly or in groups with pictures and pieces of all shapes and sizes displayed. They can be long or short and can range from formal to contemporary. They are much more creative than simply hanging assorted pieces on the wall.

Annual family photographs need not be of the traditional kind — the ones where everyone goes to the studio and poses. They can be centered around a family car, the front porch of grandma's house, in the woods or on the beach, or any place that your family loves. The end result will be one that is displayed lovingly because it not only has everyone in it, but because it conjures up great memories. After all, what makes you feel the best: standing in a sterile studio that you are visiting for the first time or standing on the beach where you spent some of the best days of your life?

A theme can be anything: a room decorated in a certain decor, a group of friends that have something in common, a generation of family members — whatever it is that you want to focus on. Here, the four generations of this family are the theme to which the entire room is decorated. The framed piece is the focal point, but in addition are the candlestick holders that each of the first three generations used in their wedding ceremonies and the handmade quilt over the couch. The books that each loved to have read to them as a child are stacked neatly in the bookcase.

We have a family room in our home that is decorated as a '50s diner. We purchased simple frames to hang around our Coke® memorabilia. It can become a great family activity to select or make frames that go with any theme!

This framing technique enables you to utilize the entire set of "proofs" from a particular photo shoot. Displaying them in a sequence or series can provide the viewer a glimpse of the many moods and expressions from the shoot.

When anyone walks into a room where a piano sits, it is evident that this setting is one of prominence, both in the decor and in the family life-style. Pianos bring to mind endless images and sounds — the hours of sitting unenthusiastically practicing, the family gathered around singing Christmas carols, the notes missed on a new piece, and the moving melodies played by a young family virtuoso. Pianos create the perfect environment for family photos and memorabilia.

At left: This couple used the music sheets of the songs played at their wedding for the background, and then mounted their wedding photograph on the top. It is a beautiful piece that creates memories in pictures and notes as well.

Frames can be made in all shapes and sizes and, with a little imagination, used for almost anything. This multiple frame was constructed so it could be a clothing or coat rack. It can be placed inside the back door or someplace less used. The clothing hung on it can be worn daily or that which was worn long ago when you were little and used to go fishing with grandpa.

It is fairly common for most of us to misplace our keys, so why not purchase or build a special "key box" to hold all of the necessary — and some not so necessary — family keys. It can be designed so the door is a frame in which a photograph of one or all family members is standing in front of a much loved car.

Having a family reunion, a large gathering of high school friends, or dinner at a wedding reception? In place of name cards, why not put childhood photos of those that are to be seated there or of the bride and groom? It is a great way to add memories and endless hours of conversation to the evening meal.

unique & unusual

If you stop to think about it for a minute, almost anything can be used to frame a picture. Here a photograph of "mom and dad" was placed inside the glass side of a contemporary lantern, and one was given to each of the children. It is fun to display such "framing" anywhere and everywhere.

All of us, children especially, love to look at pictures of themselves, family, and friends. But because they grow so quickly and their "tastes" change almost daily, a technique needs to be created to quickly and inexpensively fit their changing life-styles and needs. In our son's bedroom, we constructed a headboard out of chain link fence and purchased an old school locker to "hide" his clothes and collected treasures. They are both the perfect place to clip, tape, or easily remove favorite photographs and treasures, such as blue ribbons, theater tickets, or whatever it is that kids love to collect.

Popular with today's decorators are folding screens of every style and design. They are perfect for today's mobile life-style, which is often times somewhat confined in small places. This screen is designed to display favorite photographs. It is perfect in small apartments with little wall space, in areas where something needs to be hidden, or for children's rooms where it is advisable to conceal the remnants of their daily activities. This screen allows you to enjoy only the pictures you love and "forget" about the rest!

Have a flair for the dramatic? Why not accentuate it with your favorite photograph of your daughter, wife, or girlfriend? Borrowing the commercial concept of a light box can be intriguing when used in your home. It adds a novel and dynamic way of displaying a large photograph. This particular light box was built into the wall; however, hanging light boxes are also available for purchase. The transparencies needed for this type of display application can be made from any negative, print, or transparency, and can be obtained from most custom photographic labs and digital imaging centers.

Another borrowed commercial application is used here — taking a single photograph and enlarging it in predetermined sections, which when combined, create the finished size. Each section is then spaced evenly and hung according to the desired effect. This decorating technique is perfect for entertainment and theatre rooms.

Frames need not be purchased, new, or of a traditional nature. Those that are created from "something" else are usually the most eye-catching and fun. This frame that displays favorite family snapshots is simply an old broken window that was found in a local junk store. Used in a bedroom with an outdoor gardening theme, it is absolutely the perfect addition.

Hang it on a wall, put it on an easel, or create something new. In a child's room, in place of one of the more traditional methods, why not have a favorite teddy bear or doll hold the child's favorite photograph. It will mean more to them and to you.

It seems we all love things that are tiny and this small tabletop screen is the perfect place to "hang" tiny photographs. It is a nice alternative to a traditional 8 x 10 photograph.

Frames need not always be purchased, traditional, or made by a professional. They can be fun, like this tiny blackboard with a small section removed for the picture and put on a miniature easel.

gift ideas

There is such a variety of small frames available on the market today. Some are silver, some are gold, some are molded plastic, and some are glass. This series of our favorite frames is created by Jill Schwartz from Elements©. Every year we add a series of newly designed frames to our tree with this year's photographs. The pictures are of everyone — family and friends — which truly makes the tree the central part of our Christmas decorating.

It seems we all love wreaths. We hang them everywhere for every occasion: a Christmas wreath hangs over the fireplace to enhance the sights and scents of the season, a seasonal spring wreath hangs on the door to welcome guests, an herb wreath hangs in the kitchen. This wreath can be hung anywhere at anytime because it is a traditional green wreath decorated with silk flowers and miniature colorful frames filled with pictures of family and friends.

A simple egg carton can be used as a display element. This "eggs-tra" special gift makes a great conversation piece and decorating display for the recipient.

Children love to create, and these cute little frames made from popsicle sticks are the perfect project for any rainy afternoon. What is so nice about these is that they are easy and fun, so anyone can make as many as they want. Why not give them to school friends in place of a valentine's card this year?

Placing a family photograph on any canister, jar, or tin is a fun way to share an old family recipe.

Combining a family photograph with a printed invitation on a decorated tile provides a unique gift to deliver and display.

Pictorial vignettes can be as fun and creative as the pictures themselves. In your kitchen, why not place a collection of photos on a countertop or baker's shelf and use something decorative, but untraditional, as the easel. Here we used a serving pig to hold our photographs — you might try such things as silver trays or pottery bowls half-filled with fruit.

Hungry anyone? Dried bagels as frames add flavor to any kitchen.

Work, work, work! Does it seem like that is all you ever do? Why not put your favorite photographs where you see them all day. They may be framed on the top of your desk, reproduced on your mouse pad, or, if your job is one that is unusual, like a make-up artist, they can be placed on the sides of the containers that hold your brushes or cottonballs!

The holidays are an ideal time to decorate with family photographs. A traditional holiday wreath on a door needs only to have a picture added to the center to make it a very special one.

In addition to placing the wreath on the door, the stockings should always be hung by the chimney with care; but in place of a hook or a nail, a multitude of stocking holders are now available in gift and department stores. This set of holders are sterling silver frames. The picture of the stocking's owner can be placed inside the frame so there is no question as to who's stocking it is. Before Christmas Eve, instead of hanging empty stockings, why not use them as your Christmas card holders? It is a perfect way to display this season's greetings.

Some of us have traditional Christmas trees with lights and balls and silver tinsel. We decorate a tree in every room, and in our "Coke®" room we have decorated the tree to continue the theme. The ornament frames were made by a friend to hold photographs and to resemble different "aspects" of the '50s. There is a record with a family picture for the label, there is a frame covered with tiny buttons and charms from the era, and there is one that resembles a '50s TV set that looks as though "Father Knows Best" could be on Channel 7.

Weledings are such a special time and therefore deserve very special attention — both before and after. This purchased frame was decorated with clay flowers painted with watercolors to resemble the one's the bride carried. For those who love to give that little personal touch to all they do, the decorating of frames is one of the easiest and most appreciated.

wall
to
wall

A close-up of the family bookcase shows a variety of family photographs, decorative accents, and collected memorabilia. Do not be afraid to combine styles of frames, different categories of "things," or whatever else it is you have gathered. It doesn't have to "match" — it just needs to be filled with things that mean something to you or someone else in your family.

Displaying family photographs is an art form in and of itself. To allow each "grouping" to make a statement of its own is easier than you think. Try taking several different "photographs" taken in a variety of settings — a pencil sketch, formal portraits, moments captured unaware, maybe even one taken from behind — frame each very differently and then hang one or two and place the rest on a shelf. They can overlap and have related mementos added to the group. It can be more engaging than a traditional grouping hung on the wall.

Home's not merely
four square walls,
though with pictures
hung and gilded;
Home is where
affection calls,
filled with shrines
the hearth has builded!
— Charles Swain

Frames need not always just be frames, they can double for any number of things. Here a half-frame was constructed and then weighted to become a bookend — the possibilities of design and style are endless.

Ralph Lauren has had a tremendous impact on the home decor industry and one idea that he loves to use is old suitcases for display and effect. Here a photo was taken to specifically put inside the suitcase so it appears as if the child is "on her way." It is a nice accent for a study corner or bedroom.

Groupings of family photographs can be "themed" to add interest. Why not show photos of the passage of time. Here are photos of brother and sisters the way they were then and the way they are now. Can you only imagine what they remember every time they look at those two photographs?

Now and then can also include pictures of family and friends through the years. Do not forget to frame and display special times like those of dad when he was young, mom when she had her first baby, Aunt Mary on her 70th birthday, you when you graduated from high school. The pictures should be of different times and any number of people, the frames should match the individual photos, and the events should be remembered on a daily basis.

Small vignettes of collected images can be created anywhere and everywhere and can be themed to fit any decor. For example, on this mantle, a favorite saying was stenciled and the memorabilia on the mantle top repeats the words in a variety of mediums.

Favorite family photos are not always photos of people. Some are of places or things. We have friends who love to garden and are always taking pictures of the favorite flowers they have to tenderly nurture. As a gift, we had several of their images cropped so they were close-up or macro photographs. We then placed them in a mat that had been covered in linen and wrapped with jute. The individual photographs were mounted on a double layer of foamcore. These photographs are as dear to our friends as are the ones of their family pet.

It is as if I see it
for the first time
again,
and again,
and again.

— Author Unknown

Display favorite photographs in common areas of your home that are encountered every day. In these cases, atop the family computer table or near the key plate found in the entryway.

Some memorabilia is very near and dear to our hearts — wedding invitations, flowers saved from the senior prom, the program and tickets from the World Series. These need to be placed safely and lovingly where they can be enjoyed. Have your framer make a "frame box" that "fits" the occasion. In the frame, place one of the pictures taken during the event and inside of the box place those items that you simply could not throw away.

Photo transfers are so easy to do, why not use them as a decorating theme anywhere. In a teenager's room they can be reproduced on the pillows. They can be made more formal and put on a chair in the sitting room or they can be transferred onto sheer material, made into small sachets, and put on the dressing table.

"A Signature Print" — This 5 x 7 photograph was centered on an 8 x 10 white photo sheet, leaving the borders around the photograph white, allowing friends to write personal greetings and add their signatures. This is a perfect gift to give all of your friends at a slumber party or reunion. Get one photo for each person and have everyone sign them.

differently

Display your tiniest photographs everywhere. Lay them down, put them in tiny bird nests, fill a bowl with them. Don't be afraid to put them anywhere!

memories

Families gather in the kitchen. It is always the heart of the home, so why not use it to display much loved family photographs? Every nook and cranny can be filled with photos of family gatherings, a night out with friends, a couple's retreat, whatever event it was that you want to remember. It will make this area of the home even more loved and the center of everything that is good.

My house is filled with photographs. It's my nature to save things —
to hold the moment and try to freeze it in a frame.
— Susan J. Gordon

For some, the memories of family preserved in photographs are more important than any piece of art that could be purchased at any price. Here we have filled the family bookshelf — not with books, but with our most loved family photographs. Our favorite — taken on the steps where we were married — was enlarged and placed on an easel to make it a prominent piece in the room. Not only the four of us, but visiting friends and family members spend part of their time studying, enjoying, and remembering the moments captured in these photographs.

These lighted built-in shelves are the perfect place to display photographs. They can be constructed when you build your home, or they can be added at any time. Each shelf is equipped with overhead lights to accentuate the pictures and the treasures being displayed.

display

Probably the most traditional of all places to display pictures is the fireplace mantle, and it should still never be forgotten.

The memories we collect and give brighten our lives as long as we live . . .
— Author Unknown

element three
gathering your images

Now that you have determined your decorating style, you are going to find photographs that depict that style. You will use these photographs for decorating, but you want them to virtually tell the story of your life.

gathering

When beginning to gather your photographic images, you must first decide what types of photographs you are going to use and where you will get them. Will they come from existing albums, desk frames, or from those currently on the walls? Will they be old or new? Do new ones need to be created either by yourself or professionally? What images will they be? Will they be those of family, individuals, grandparents, children, pets, places, hobbies, things, events, vintage images . . . .

When favorite pictures are kept in shoe boxes, lab envelopes, or scrapbooks, they are more difficult to share. If they are taken from these hiding places and possibly enlarged, cropped, tinted, digitally enhanced, or creatively matted and/or framed, they become more than forgotten images or mere snapshots in an album. They become works of art that evoke emotions and give life to your memories.

Who will look at all these pictures in future years?
Will a young child take them out of some boxes some day
and study them with fresh curiosity?
Will our photographs explain what we were really like or
simply acknowledge that, for a time, we were here?
— Susan J. Gordon

using existing images

Throughout the pages of this book, we will share with you concepts and examples that will generate new ideas on how to effectively, creatively, and lovingly decorate with photography.

Our suggestion is that you seize the opportunity and take the time, now, to rethink the way in which your existing photographs have been selected, framed, and displayed.

clicking new images

having new professional images taken

tell the story . . .

When gathering images, make certain you keep in mind what it is you are trying to accomplish when you determine your decorating style — and that is to select images that either:

- tell a story
- create a family showcase
- or blend with your decorative theme

Your first option, which is probably the easiest and least expensive, is to select existing images. These can come from those currently displayed on walls, those in recently compiled scrapbooks, those from old family albums, school pictures . . . .

decorating with
existing

Family farms, summer seaside cottages, or Victorian homes with gabled roofs are sometimes a large part of our family history. Why not take the photographs of these homes your hearts have never left, have them enlarged, and use them in place of a watercolor painted by an unknown painter of a place you have never been?

When existing images on the pages of your scrapbook are removed, reproduced, and framed, they make delightfully unexpected additions to your art and decorating scheme. Why not take your favorite family photographs and place them in groupings on shelves over doorways or inside tiny kitchen nooks that traditionally hold spices and wooden spoons?

images

Your second option is to click new images. This publication will not attempt to teach you how to take photographs, it is assumed that you already know how to operate the camera that you own. What is provided are some helpful hints that can make the photos you take just a little bit better than those you have taken before.

For those of you who do not want to be bothered with changing lenses and filters or using a tripod, your camera of choice should be of the "point and shoot" variety.

decorating with
new images

If you are using a "point and shoot" type camera, here are a few tips to help you achieve the best possible photo:

- use a quality camera that has an autofocus "zoom" lens and a red-eye reducing feature

- use the appropriate film for the lighting conditions that are present — for example, use a higher ISO film (400 speed) for low light conditions and lower ISO (100 speed) for bright light conditions, where color saturation and detail are critical

- cloudy, overcast days provide the best lighting

- always try to photograph children at their eye level

- find a good photo lab that has a reputation for quality photographs as some express labs may not

If you are a photo enthusiast and you own a 35mm camera with removable lenses and other accessories, here are a few tips to assure successful results:

- plan your shoot in advance

- determine the best time of day for the proper lighting which best suits your mood and feel for the photographs to be taken — generally, early mornings and just before sunset are best

- choose the right lens for the job — for example, a scenic mountain range looks best photographed with a wide-angle type lens

- when shooting a portrait, a longer focal length lens helps compress the background, making it a little "out of focus," which in turn emphasizes the face without yielding to any "distortion" like a wide angle lens could

with a polarizer   without a polarizer

wide-angle

A simple quiet moment shared between two can be captured forever with the same emotions and illusions that were felt while standing there. A wide-angle lens allows you to capture not only the moment, but the surroundings that made that moment spectacular.

It is sometimes as important to capture the immensity of a "picture" as it is the focal point itself. Imagine the altered impact of this photo if the barn were up close and excluded the grandeur of the distant mountain range. Such majestic images can be easily captured with a wide-angle lens, then enlarged and hung in a den or study.

- when using backlighting, try using the flash on your camera as a source of fill even in broad daylight — for example, on the beach you would either have the sun at the back or to the side of the subject being taken, then the flash will fill in the shadows on the faces
- try some different "special effect filters" — diffusion, star effects, colored gradients, etc. — each can add that little extra ambiance to any image when used properly and not overdone
- use a polarizing filter for your outdoor images — it will provide more dramatic skylines and remove unwanted reflections

professional
decorating with images

Coming from a professional, this advice could possibly be construed as biased; but it is known that there are some things a professional can do that most cannot — and shooting great portraits is one of them. As you will see in the upcoming "professional gallery," true artistry in imaging is a special talent. It is a gift and a finely-tuned skill that is rare. When you want to have something truly wonderful created for your home, seek out the professional that best fits your style and taste.

When working with a professional, you should, first and foremost, look at the studio's work and learn about their personnel. Go to the studio, meet the staff (photographer, associate photographer(s), studio designer or stylist, and studio manager), and familiarize yourself with the studio facilities. Most importantly, talk with the photographer that will be taking your photographs. Do your personalities complement each other? Does their creative style fit your needs? Is creativity and imagination evident in their work? Is the quality offered that which you desire and expect? Is their pricing in line with your budget? Finally, one of the most important aspects of all, does their work tell a story? An affirmative "yes" must be the answer to all of these questions before making the investment in a fine portrait created by a professional.

Once you have decided upon a studio, you should arrange a consultation with the photographer who will be creating your images. Most reputable studios will provide this as part of their service, but if not, take the initiative to set one up. More than anything else, this appointment will determine the success or failure of the photo session. This meeting should cover all of the details involved with the shoot — the photography style that is expected, the setting location (indoors or outdoors), appropriate clothing choices, the availability of make-up and hair stylists, props and sets that will be needed, whether or not pets are involved, and whether or not hobbies are to be incorporated into the shoot. All expectations and requirements for both parties must be covered and everyone must make certain they understand each other's expectations.

planning

preparation

After all that goes before the photograph, it is important to frame and display the finished piece in a prominent place. Here, this professional photograph was cropped in high-fashion style and placed in front of a light that was added for effect.

element four

finishing and framing ideas

With your decorating style determined, your photographic images selected, and your special effects applied, it is time to determine the style of frame that will be used.

The first aspect of framing is to select a professional who can create the finished effect for the wall-mounted or tabletop frames that you desire. Similar to choosing a professional photographer, we recommend you visit several frame shops and review the quality and composition of their work.

Keep in mind that the framing selections you will be making for your photo projects should coordinate with your decorating style — thus reflecting your personal style, your life-style, and your display style.

Alternatives to professional framing are ready-made frames available in an amazing variety of colors, sizes, shapes, mediums, and price ranges. They can be purchased with or without mats and the number and size of photographs that can fit within each frame varies.

When selecting a frame, you will begin by choosing a moulding style. Look for size, shape, color, finish, material, etc. Moulding styles vary from contemporary, Victorian, or shadow box; narrow or wide profiles; stained, painted, or decorated; wood, metal, or moulded frames.

After deciding upon which moulding will be used, you will determine whether a mat is desired. If so, the mat can be single, double, plain, hand-cut, in coordinating or contrasting colors, hand-painted, paper covered, etc. Whatever choices are made, make certain the mat enhances the photographed images and does not overpower or detract from that which is most important.

finishing

decorating with frames

Framing can be ornate, yet simply dignified. Here, a plain frame with carved corners and no mat makes a quiet statement of sophistication. Even though it could stand alone in the decorating theme, a collection of objects were added. Two sconces, candles, or lights on either side of a picture is a nice added effect, as are the identical topiaries. The mantle grouping is now complete with the framed photograph being the focal point.

This frame was actually purchased as a mirror in a department store. The mirror was removed and the enlarged photo was inserted. It was important to the designer that the frame be ornate, unusual, and massive. A professional framer could not create such a piece and ready-made frames with these qualifications are difficult to locate. This piece is now one of the most outstanding design components and the focal point of the room.

decorating with
professional

A formal decorating style requires formal treatment of photography and displayed here is a beautifully done formal family photograph flanked by individual shots taken of the family members. The ornate piece above the large framed piece adds interest and accentuates the formal feel of the pictoral arrangement.

A remarkable photograph deserves nothing less than a delicate, yet noteworthy, mat. To accentuate the silky colors in the photograph, the mat was created with handmade papers — one of which was created with a watercolor wash. This piece is definitely one that the mother wanted surrounded by beautiful things and placed in a prominent section of her formal living room.

framing

frame it

Gifts made by hand and given from the heart are always those that are treasured most. Frames can be embellished with needlework, such as ribbon embroidery. Old crocheted pieces from grandmother's doilies can also be added for a look that will be enjoyed and cherished everyday.

These quilt frames are our favorite. One holds a special photograph, one holds a piece of Aunt Mary's quilt that kept us warm through winter months, and the third is left unfilled to hang on the wall until the next memory that is shared and celebrated.

This cross-stitched frame, made to hold an old family wedding photo, was created and given by a friend who adds her special touch to everything. It is delicate, beautifully done, and much loved.

element five

applying photographic treatments and effects

Now that you have gathered the images that will be used in your decorating schemes, you are ready to choose the specific photographic treatment or effect that can be used to enhance, change, beautify, or modify some of your selected images.

A few examples of such photographic treatments are black and white, colorized black and white, hand-colored black and white, old photograph restoration, canvas mounting, digitally manipulated images, and photo edges. In this chapter we will discuss these sometimes simple, sometimes complex photographic treatments that can slightly modify or add total enhancement to your photographs.

applying

If you have worked with a professional to create your images, in all likelihood these services can be provided by the studio. If you are working with existing images or images you have created yourself, these services are available through qualified professional photo labs everywhere.

Omega
UNIVERSAL
Variable Condenser Lamphouse
ffects
digital
imagi
out
color
chnique
b&w
Seconds
estoration
scannin

You will find a very simple and common technique that has regained popularity over the past few years is the traditional black-and-white print. Its classic and timeless look make it a very powerful display media.

Creative variations of the traditional black-and-white theme can be toning (brown or light sepia), colorizing, or hand-coloring.

decorating using different

types of images

The rich and the famous oftentimes have pictures taken of themselves and duplicated in "Andy Warhol"-type ways. Why not take your daughter's portrait this year, crop it dramatically, change the colors, duplicate it, and hang it in your living room. She is beautiful, you love her so, and it is the perfect way to accent your new contemporary decorating scheme.

Hand-colored black-and-white photographs add a hint of yesteryear and can easily be "colored" using several different techniques. These techniques range from using traditional oils and pastels on archival quality black-and-white prints, to using "paint pens" available from various manufacturers. In addition, your computer can be used, using programs such as Photoshop® or PhotoPaint®, to achieve the same look. This technique is interpretive, so have fun!

Daughters grow and change and grow and change and grow and change. Their pictures in each stage should be framed and placed on a nightstand so they never really change at all!

hand-colored

A classic, traditional finishing technique, worthy of your consideration, and borrowed from famous painters throughout history, is the "canvas mount", which has been used by photographers for years to emulate the master's painted canvas. It is available from professional photographers and from most custom photographic labs.

Traditionally, pictures are hung on the wall in expected places. To emphasize the importance of this year's portrait, why not display it on an easel in an unexpected location — like at the bottom of a winding staircase. It will become a center of conversation and the focal point of your decorating.

Digital Imaging. What is it and what does it mean? This section will be touching on some of the amazing effects that almost anyone can achieve using the "power" of a computer. With the personal computer becoming an ever-increasing facet of our lives, using programs like Adobe Photoshop®, Corel Photo-Paint®, and many others, you now have the capability for unlimited creativity in your own photography.

An elite group of professionals have embraced this technology from its infancy because of the advantages and dramatic effects that can be achieved by using digital imaging. Their computer expertise allows freedoms and options never known before and the computer itself has forever changed the way in which professionals and amateurs alike will create photographic images.

A custom photographic lab and digital imaging center can provide you as the consumer with many computerized image manipulations utilizing state-of-the-art digital equipment and technical expertise. However, if you choose not to use their services, it is necessary for you to understand a few of the basics in creating digital images. Though this is not a "how-to" book, you will be provided with many examples and descriptions of how some of them were created and what is required to create digital images of your own.

If you have a desire to learn more about this exciting technology, looking into area colleges and universities that offer classes on specific software programs and applications is suggested.

Your first decision in quality digital imaging (DI) is choosing a platform — PC or MAC? This is the age old question that every person we know debates as much as they do politics. Our digital imaging center prefers the MAC for its ease of use and powerful graphics capabilities. However, a PC can, in most cases, do the job equally well.

digital imaging options

technology

With the age of computer imaging and unlimited possibilities of reproduction, "art" in photography is easier to achieve than ever before. Here, the annual children's photograph was enhanced to look like an oil painting and then enlarged to an overly dramatic size. It was then hung as the focal point in the entry way for all who enter to see.

Once you have established your choice of computer and have selected your digital imaging center, you will need to make certain your computer can handle several factors associated with digital imaging. First and foremost is file size. To create quality photographic digital images, resolution is the key — and high resolution means large file size.

The old axiom of "garbage in — garbage out" applies to photographic digital imaging. Therefore, it is necessary to get it into the computer at the quality and resolution needed because

BEVAN WHITEAR

the computer cannot enhance the quality of the existing images.

To adequately handle large files, the processor speed is vital. Processor speed is usually referred to in megahertz (Mhz) — the higher Mhz your computer has, the faster it will be. The faster the processor, the quicker it allows you to process large amounts of information. This makes doing numerous functions in these complex graphics programs quick and efficient.

BEVAN WHITEAR

The effect above was achieved by merging two separate photographs into one using several Adobe Photoshop® effects. A portion of the first image, in this case the bottom right window pane, was selected and deleted, leaving a position open into which the second photograph, a mother and her daughter, was placed.

At left: The digital imaging manipulations of the photograph at left utilized Adobe Photoshop® to vignette and soften its edges. In addition, a thin-lined border was added in a complementary color.

As stated earlier, to achieve "photographic quality" results, you will need to be using high-resolution images. At least 300 pixels per inch (PPI) is recommended for the finished size of your image. For example, an 8 x 10 print at 300 PPI would result in a 20 megabyte (MB) file. This size of file requires an external device that can transport large amounts of data quickly and easily.

While working with graphics and image processing, RAM is a critical component to the process. Therefore, you should have as much RAM as you can afford — like money, you can never have too much! With the cost of RAM becoming so affordable it is not out of the question to have at least 128 MB.

Your next item of consideration is the size of the hard drive being used and the presence of a video card. Your hard drive should be in the 3–4 gigabyte (GB) range to handle the storage of your images, and you should have at least a 17" monitor interfaced with a high-resolution video card. Again, bigger is better when choosing a hard drive and video card.

This photograph was first scanned in black and white, then converted to a sepia-toned image. To achieve the hand-painted look, a dry-brush filter was applied.

The high-contrast look and feel of this photograph was achieved by using a combination of Adobe Photoshop® filters and effects. By experimenting, a myriad of looks can be achieved.

input tools

On the following pages are several simple techniques that can be utilized to make your photographs true works of art.

The first example is commonly referred to as a "giclée" fine art print. This product is offered through fine portrait studios and various custom photo labs throughout the world. This service is provided by professional photographers and is available to anyone. The samples in this book were produced by Strauss Peyton Imaging.

A giclée starts with a traditional photographic image scanned from any negative, print, or transparency at a high resolution. Once scanned, the digital file is then artistically manipulated to varying degrees of intensity to resemble that of a watercolor painting. When the file is finished, it is digitally printed on artist-quality watercolor paper. This process takes the attributes of a photograph and couples them with the beauty and delicacy of a watercolor to produce an image like no other.

Additional artistic effects, which can be created on your home computer or are available through custom photographic labs and digital imaging centers, can be achieved by utilizing numerous image-editing software programs.

raw image — no manipulation

subtle — edges only

moderate — background and edges

intensive — entire image manipulation

artistic effects

106

Some of us feel more comfortable when surrounded with the traditional, yet need that touch of the nontraditional to make everything just perfect. Here a photograph was needed to hang above the couch, but it was taken in grandmother's flower garden and then enhanced by digital imaging to soften the edges. It is a very subtle nontraditional effect that is just enough.

A year from now, you may wish you had captured today.

We all love make-believe — whether we are six or sixty. To capture the moments of pretend that live forever in our hearts is not only important, but relatively simple to do. Allow yourself or your children to "dress-up," have the perfect picture of a time fantasy taken, soften the edges to make it dreamy, and display it on an easel in a prominent place. It will instantly recreate the fantasy every time you look at it.

Warm Wishes and Happy Holidays
the Collier Family

We live in a society that prevents us from keeping in touch with our family and friends as often as we should. Because of this, it is important to keep in touch in a number of ways. One very special way is to have the family picture taken annually and have it made into your Christmas card or just a simple greeting card that can be sent just to say "you are missed and thought of daily." Have each family member write a short note on the inside and instantly an everyday greeting card can say so much more.

greeting cards

109

Where do you put your Christmas cards — especially those that should go in an album because they are this year's pictures of family and friends. Why not display them throughout the holiday season in a basket on the living room coffee table. When the season is over, you can cut the photo from the Christmas greeting, remount it on a piece of mat board, and place it back in the basket with little bits of spring.

restore

The above is the original photograph that is aged, faded, and cracked.

The above is the retouched original photograph. Once it was scanned at a high resolution, the color balance and densities were adjusted and the cracks, scratches, and imperfections were cleaned up, using the Adobe Photoshop® rubberstamp tool, which allows you to clone areas.

The ability to restore treasured "old" photographs that have been handed down over the years, but have faded or been torn or damaged in some way, is one of the greatest uses for digital imaging.

In minutes, your PC allows you to do what used to take many hours at great expense using traditional techniques. The image above was scanned and restored in less than one hour.

Family photographs should indeed be kept in family albums, but they should also be duplicated and exhibited in places of importance. Your grandparents or their grandparents were the foundation for all that is good in your family and their pictures should be placed where they can be remembered. In addition to the vintage photographs, placing them in a vintage frame seems to put the time in the proper setting.

Vintage photographs where no original negative exists can be copied, creating a new negative, then enlarged and framed to add nostalgia to any decor. When deciding which old family photographs to include in your decorating scheme, think about a variety of combinations. For example: your grandmother and grandfather on their wedding day and a companion piece of your mother's baby picture. Or how about your mother and father when they were children and then again on their wedding day. In this way, your vintage photographs tell a story that most in your family are unfamiliar with.

heritage

At times I can almost feel the presence of my ancestors —
a gentle, guiding touch from those who have gone before.
— Author Unknown

decorating using

nontraditional

You can easily add creative and distinctive edge effects to all your photographs. These edge effects can help enhance the tone and feeling of an image by giving the photograph added dimension and character. These effects can be achieved by utilizing a variety of software applications such as Photo/Graphic Edges® from Auto F/X Corporation.

This technique can be coupled with favorite quotes, sayings, and other graphic elements to create personalized sentimental images. This concept is becoming so popular that our studio is creating an endless variety of these images in a new line we have named MEMOIRS.

A sister is both your mirror - and your opposite.

Megan & Erika Chambers '97

photographic

Future Hall of Famer...

memoirs

When somewhat traditional photographs are manipulated with special edge effects and sayings are added, they become even more personalized and treasured. Such additions can make giving and displaying family photographs even more meaningful. Giving grandma and grandpa their grandson's picture with his "hopes for the future" written underneath makes a perfect addition to their bedside table. Because they are so far away, it is nice that in this way they can "see" their firstborn grandson the last moment of every day and first thing as their new day begins.

techniques

Many of us spend more time in our offices at our desks than we do at home with our families, so it is only logical that we would place our favorite photographs on our desks where we can see them all day, every day. To make these photographs even more meaningful, thoughts, messages, or prayers can be printed underneath.

What is more important to any of us than the memories of our children when they were young? If this is truly the way you feel, you will want to make decorative groupings in your home and center them around your most beloved photos. These treasures should not be relegated only to the pages of family albums, but distinctively placed so everyone might "relive" a few of the memories.

It is a great privilege to present this professional gallery featuring some of the world's finest portrait artists and image makers. This gallery of photographic images is presented with the hope of inspiring personal creative ideas, as well as confirming the concept that utilizing the talents of great professionals produces extraordinary images that not only enhance and beautify your decorative theme, but become works of art and treasured heirlooms. When a photograph has been carefully planned, prepared for, and brought to fruition, the results become more than ordinary. They become the vehicle for displaying the true form of the subject(s) being photographed in the moods and settings of the moment, ultimately capturing that which is most important — the true essence of the image.

Professional Photographers of America
THE WORLD'S GREAT STORYTELLERS SM

DENNIS CLOUTIER

The Sirene

Sometimes
words
just
aren't
enough.
— Author
Unknown

Each of our children has a special quality we love or a personal fantasy that they live time and time again. Whether it be a welcome childlike smile or a dream of saving the bewitched prince, each should be recorded so that it never be forgotten. In these photographs, childhood moments have been captured in ways that make these childhood photographs pieces of collectable art. They are simply children whose cherished images have been "graphically and artistically manipulated" to make the fantasy real.

Paradise

Water lily

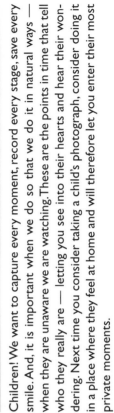

Children! We want to capture every moment, record every stage, save every smile. And, it is important when we do so that we do it in natural ways — when they are unaware we are watching. These are the points in time that tell who they really are — letting you see into their hearts and hear their wondering. Next time you consider taking a child's photograph, consider doing it in a place where they feel at home and will therefore let you enter their most private moments.

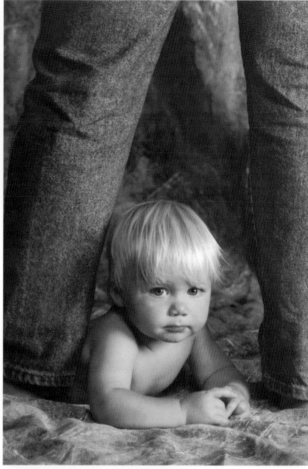

Some children love the quiet of the expected and some thrive on the recognition and responses of the theatrical. A professional photographer can create and capture these special moment's of pretend in a way that will freeze the childhood dreams of fantasy, stardom, or excitement forever. Childhood photographs are infinitely more fun if occasionally they are unexpected and dictated by the children.

KEVIN DILLEY for HAZEN IMAGING, INC.

Life ÷ Moments = Memories
— Author Unknown

RANDY COLLIER

It's essential that a part of you
not grow up.
Childhood wonder gives us
our spirit and our beauty.

— Author Unknown

STEVE MACKLEY

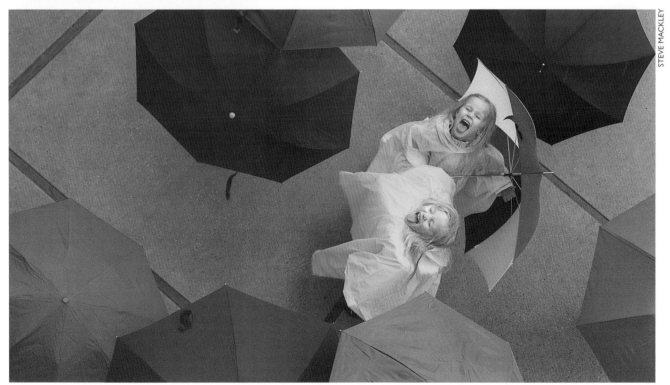

STEVE MACKLEY

ALAN GIBBY

Families . . . they are first in our hearts. The very center of our universe, and even though they remain constant, they change in the blink of an eye. It is so important to capture on an annual basis the stages through which the family members travel. If you don't, you will forget how your youngest son looked the summer before graduation or the year your daughter's hair looked remarkably similar to the family dog's. These family photographs should be taken, not always in a photographer's studio, but in a natural surrounding that is part of who you are. You are not structured sets with contrived backgrounds, you are hikers by your favorite stream, boaters on your favorite lake, or car aficionados in front of the family roadster.

JOHN SINCLAIR

DENNIS HAMMON

MICHAEL TAYLOR

MICHAEL TAYLOR

DENNIS CLOUTIER

BOB MALONEY

Each of us has an inner side. One that is somewhat different than the everyday. A professional photographer can capture that somewhat hidden soul in a way no one else can. Some of us see a small part of ourselves as quiet and reflective, or maybe sexy and seductive, or perhaps just the way we look when occasionally we get all dressed up in our very finest. It is this "other side" that should be seen and photographed just once in a while.

MICHAEL TAYLOR

Who are you really? The adored family pet? The boy with his constant companion? A grandfather who is the unpretentious cornerstone of the family? Whoever you may be, it is important to be photographed as you really are so that as life changes and you unknowingly become someone else, you will be able to remember who you were.

DON BUSATH

DRAKE BUSATH

Your wedding — truly one of the most important days of your life. You will never again be more beautiful, never again be so filled with hope for the future, never again be so everything — nervous, happy, emotional, ecstatic, frantic . . . Each and all of these should be recorded for you and your generations that will follow. Why not take your wedding pictures where he proposed, in a quiet moment shared by just the two of you, or in a setting you love that is as spectacular as the day?

contributors

We extend our appreciation to the following companies for their contributions:

Adobe Systems, Inc.

Artist Touch Framing
(801) 394-7003

Auto F/X Corporation

Classic Trends

Corel Corporation

Eastman Kodak®

Exposures® (Catalog) —
a Division of Miles Kimball
(800) 572-5750

Strauss Peyton Imaging
(800) 786-7752

We wish to acknowledge our colleagues who so graciously donated some of the sample images that appear in our gallery section and throughout this book:

Don Busath, Master Photographer
(801) 364-6645

Drake Busath, Master Photographer
(801) 364-6645

Randy Collier, Master Photographer
(801) 571-6369

Kevin Dilley for Hazen Imaging
(800) 279-1922

Hanson Fong, Master Photographer
(415) 433-7994

Alan Gibby, Master Photographer
(801) 394-1644

Dennis Hammon, Master Photographer
(208) 745-8518

J. Ryne Hazen, CPP
(800) 279-1922

Evelyn Hymas
(208) 544-2021

David Labrum for Busath Photography
(801) 364-6645

Steve Mackley
(435) 753-5163

Bob Maloney, Master Photographer
(208) 734-9969

Lisa Jane Murphy, Master Photographer
(713) 699-8128

Scott Soderberg
(801) 579-6125

John Sinclair

Michael Taylor, Master Photographer
(818) 577-8999

Gary Weitzeil
(801) 829-3673

Bevan Whitear, Master Photographer
(801) 540-4010

Photography Locations:

The homes of Dave and Diane Ault, Paul and Eva Butler, Dave and Linda Durbano, and Ryne and Teresa Hazen.

The showrooms of Classic Trends Design, Kaylene's Interiors, and R.C. Willey.

HERE'S HOW . . .

Additional information and detailed instructions on specific projects and techniques, can be obtained by visiting our website at:

www.hazenphoto.com

127

index